EVERYTHNG IS ENERGY AND ENERGY IS EVERYTHING !!

POSITIVE OR NEGATIVE EVERYTHING IS ENERGY !!

RUPALI BHATTACHARYA

ISBN 979-888546891-6

Contents

CHAPTER ONE

EVERYTHING IS ENERGY !!

If I ask you Whom you want as your Soul mate "positive smiling face, good energy person or otherwise sulking face , negative vibe person

Let me ask you one more question, if you had to employ people whom you would hire or choose ??? "Positive, good energy people or negative people

Your answers in both the cases would be "positive , smiling face, good energy people" .Does it ring bells guys ????

What are you afraid of Guys ???

Cameras, facebook, phones tablets, laptops ???

Universe has big cameras, Universe is watching you every single moment of every single day. Its watching you how you show up ? How you are ? Its watching you what vibration you are ?

Its responding directly to every single moment of you

Universal cameras hears everything you say. It hears everything you say. It hears everythinng you think, it responses to everything you feel, it observes how you act ? what you do?

People call it karma happening in every single moment.

If you want to achieve positive results in anything,be it personnel life or professional life, anything you do, speak , think and act positive all three has to be in alignment.

Same goes for achieving your dreams and then Miracles starts happening, thats why we say ,"Everything is Energy" !!

CHAPTER TWO

"LIFE IS A MIRRIOR"

Suppose there is a man in some energy field positive or negative. He would see life accordingly to his belief. And would refelect back what is inside him, that is why it is said that "LIFE IS A MIRRIOR", it reflects what you are inside.

Some beliefs which come from our parents may not Resonate with us anymore. Understanding Everything in life is fundamentally neutral, it has no inbuilt meaning.

Everyone and Everything that shows up in our life is a reflection of something that is happening inside of us.

We impose meaning, definitions. We impose language,what happens in a story? and how we interpret ? what meaning we give it to ?

Thats why people sometimes with no hands and no legs do wonders based on their belief system. People will feel what you feel.

Interpret things Positively and positive results would come out in Reality.

We gona pick up information out of so much out there equal to Defeinition and Language of beliefs we have and exactly that would be reflected back.

We are all connected to everyone ,every single person on this planet.We are all connected to everyone else.Thats why when you put out, you get back Reflective Consciousness.

At greater spiritual level.We are all one. What you putting out, you get back, thats why we say"Do good and good is bound to come back to you .And breathing in reality is a reflection, that why we say it " life is a mirrior"!!

Change the way of interpretation and you will change your life!!

CHAPTER THREE

SELF TRANSFORMATION TO FUTURE SELF

There are three steps to it

AWARENESS

Awareness about Yourself, Sometimes it is uncomfortable at first because we are so used to being in our own identity Box and Identity is not static or fixed.Once we know this ,its almost like a whole new world of opportunities and possibilities opens up.

for example: a person having trauma can only be healed if he knows he is into it.

next step involves your Reasoning

REASONING

next step involves your Reasoning.

Reasoning allows your "Beliefs to Shift". Reasons we give things is a direct reflection of your reality, for example :Reasoning helps to heal, what meaning we give, it leads to spiritual awakening.

CHOOSE NEW IDENTITY

Third step involves choose new identity that resonates and start wiring that new Identity through Daily practice of being into New Identit.Many powerful techniques like Visualization Affirmations and Meditations are of great help to it

TRUST UNIVERSE

Fourth step is to Trust Universe

Five mantras/Affirmations that will change your Life

These Vibrations become you...

1)who am I not to trust Universe

2) I am what I want and I attract what I am

3) Everything that I think is already into existence

4) Its already done Everything is Energy and Energy is Everything

5) I am a magnet to Money Fame and love

6)I Surrender to the creator you the powerful universe and will let you work your magic in divine timing to deliver what is already Mine

CHAPTER FOUR

STOP OVER THINKING

Three ways to start actually living !!

(i))SHIFT YOUR PATTERN

Snap out of negativity

We Create more negativity when we focus on it,as the old proverb says where ever attention goes energy flows is absolutely correct,when you think speak and discuss negatively.It would for sure enhance in your life.Because we reflect what we feel.

That's why its very important,think of good times, some holiday trips, some memories which would remind of some hilarious memories.

Just snap out of it

FIVE HAZZARDS OF BEING INTO POSITIVE ENERGY

1. *Get rid of scarcity mindset.*
2. *Lack of emotions, zeal, zest in life.*
3. *Find your tribes/environment,vibes,positive spirits,creative circle*
4. *Lack of action*

Confidence building comes when you get out of comfort zone,its necessary to take actions for particular target to achieve

5) Not with in your destiny path

Real inner calling or Ego or Doing things for the sake of doing it

(ii) BREATHE

Be calm, feel the Present moment Now,Relax feel your existence and you will realize there is no problem in the immediate new, meditate if possible, to break the spell of negativity, stress, worries. It is said when you meditate major to major mental health issues get rectify

(iii) FOCUS ON THE NOW

Be totally present in the now.

This is the only moment which matters,bow down,have gratitude for the air we breathe,food we eat. This present moment i.e now creates future,so keep taking action in this present moment "now". Your daily routine would govern your future life.

For bright fabulous future have fabulous imagination and take action accordingly but right now having vivid memory of past and fabulous imagination of future is the key to living a peaceful and fruitful life.

Be what never loose your wonderfulness because someone or something in your life.(Never)

ALWAYS BE YOUR WONDERFUL SELF

NO MATTER WHAT

CHAPTER FIVE

MEDITATION

Have you ever unlocked the main door and entered your home after a vaccation of two or four weeks ? YOU are greeted by the smell of a closed home ,a sweet smell of dust. You throw yourself on the couch and let out a big sigh.You say"Home Sweet Home"!!

No matter how beautiful the Vaccation might be,after a while you start missing home.You want to get back to a familiar setting.

The same goes for our soul as well.Our Body is not its permanent home.Our Individual consciousness is eternally trying to merge in the supreme consciousness, It wants to go home.The soul wants to go back to its source.This is the most fundamental law of nature, of creation and destruction.

Everything must return to its source.Our body may be temporary,our minds conditioned,our consciousness a wary traveller,but our soul knows where it belongs.Thats why every person at some point in their lives is forced to think about the meaning of their lives.

Everyone,who's experienced even a minute of fullfillment, embarks on a journey greater than their individual existence.That journey could be the path of Einstein or the passion of christ,it could be the path of Buddha or the moksha of Vedas.

We may have forgotten our true nature but our soul-eternal and unblemished wants to go home.Until you show it the way,the ruthlessness in life will not go away.No pleasure or relationship can offer you permanent fullfillment because we are all on a vaccation, and we are missing home.

MEDITATION IS GOING HOME

It is going back to your source,where you belong,so that you are no longer what people tell you who you are,what the world has made you to believe or even what you think of yourself.Instead, it is to discover yourself, to get to your primal source from where Bliss,Happiness and joy flow constantly.It is to discover your original home,without the furniture of jealosuy,covetousness,envy, hatred. A Home with no walls of ego and anger, a place where your soul rest in peace, where consciousness flows unimpeded like the gentle ganges murmuring on a sunny day.

When you get home,you'll realize that your room of bliss has always been there.Its your home,after all......

CHAPTER SIX

KARMA

There are three types of karma

1) Your past life Experience (Sanchita)

2) Result of your action on this life(Prarabdha)

3) Future karma that you build (Again)

Every suffering was given to an Individual only because he/ she is able to stand it.

Some people get more or less suffering because of

1) We are working on karma we developed in past life.

2) We are working on karma we developed in this life.

so each suffering we get either it's sickness or unconditional love, poorness, etc

It all happens because of these 2 reasons,karma is not a destiny or punishment.It is only the action that has energy in it. And by the law of existence it comes back to you in different life Aspects but with the Same energy that we ones performed.

You act on a specific frequency.Each minute your thoughts feelings habits goals it all has a vibrational shade and this is how we attract the same vibration, and the same cases in our life.

So lets act on high frequency (heart center level) and life will be already wonderful.

Burn your karma with changing your reaction on negativity.

Forgive all people who hurt you, forgive yourself.Destroy your dependencies. Develop unconditional love to every alive being.

Care about environment as you care about your own house. With each Action we build our next outcome.

lets not fail it....

CHAPTER SEVEN

Daily Routine

"You'll never change your life until you change something you do Daily."

The secret of your success is found in your daily routine". How will you do one thing is how you do everything. Doing the bare minimum, with no intention to grow like an auto pilot will not give any results because that energy is contagious what we feel, people feel it. That mentality will come out so doing what you love, passionate about with 100% involvement is the key to raise your vibration. Because external reality is the reflection of internal reality. And when your vibration is high you will attract people and things which resonate with you and thus would be able to manifest your dreams into reality

Your personality is personal reality of how you act, feel and think, if all of them is in alignment you would achieve what ever you aim for and secret is never "want in life but feel act and think as if you have it already.

Your outer reality is just reflection of your inner reality. Be that version which you want to manifest or aim for.

Be that version that already has the money love and success and decideds that's who you are .Now carry yourself ,body language, gestures accordingly.

Some of the activities followed by very successful people

1. *Wake up early*
2. *Exercise/yoga*
3. *Meditate for atleast 10 minutes*
4. *Be a reader*
5. *Manage stress through extreme sports*
6. *Plan the minutes of your day*
7. *Spend time alone in the morning to set priorities for the day*
8. *Read something for pleasure*
9. *Make most of your commute*
10. *Never leave any emails unread*
11. *Smile and talk to strangers*
12. *Eat dinner as a family every night, with no electronics allowed.*
13. *Leave your phone on the kitchen counter at night*
14. *Do consistently one thing you love daily.*
15. *Add value to people*
16. *Be joyful*
17. *Jump into new*
18. *Forgive people for "to err is to human".*

CHAPTER EIGHT

HOW TO BE JOYFUL !!

Imagine buying a new shirt and wanting people to comment on it. The wanting of people to comment on it repels them from doing so because no one wants to be manipulated or controlled. When your cup is full and you don't need the compliments you'll get them.(paradox)

When do you truly feel well ?When you are very happy

Depressions means your life energies has become low and staid.

Happiness means your life energies has become exuberant.

Your life energies are happening in a more exuberant way than normally. Everybody has been happy but the problem is they are not able

to maintain it ,that's all.

So you don't have to enforce any resolutions upon yourself. A business man keeps accounts to see weather they are at profit side or at loss. Similarly we should keep account about our joyness weather we are at loss or profit for every day and every month every year.

It is only when we are at acute loss we check on our joyfulness

1. *How joyful are you and how much joy do you give to people around you?*

This you can keep accounts. People are keeping accounts of their money as if they're going to carry it with them. The real wealth of life is how joyful you are, how wonderful is your experience of life?

Joy is not a goal by itself but it's a necessary ambience for life.If you don't set this one ambiance then whatever you have is just going waste.

1. *Remember it's a brief life.*

Tomorrow if you wake up in the morning, is it not a fanstastic thing, because over a million people will not wake up tomorrow morning.You are living with an idea that you are immortal, you are not conscious of your mortality.

If you were conscious, would you have time to crib ?

Would you have time to fight with somebody. Would you have time to do some rubbish with your life?

You would absolutely not

3. *Take charge of your happiness*

It is your karma, that means its your making. You will have to

Understand "this is my making, entirely my making, the moment you see it, you have the ability to change it.

Everything that is not you keep it aside mentally, what you are will be there, practice every day, karma means your action, love is nothing but sweetness of your emotions.

Five minutes every day for love.What is a love affair ?

You are trying to make somebody who is not a part of you, a part of yourself emotionally. This is a love affair.

If you do it consciously, we call it yoga !!

For 5 minutes everyday, go sit with something that does not mean anything to you, may be a tree or a pebble or a worm or an insect. After sometime you will find you can look upon it with as much love as you hold for your wife, husband, mother, child or dog.

May be the worm does not know this, if you can look at everything lovingly this world will become a beautiful phenomenon for you.

You realize love is not something that you do, it is the way you are.

Do a daily life audit , keep everything aside before going to bed,

Rememmber it's a brief life

Take charge of your happiness ...

Five minutes every day for love !!

CHAPTER NINE

PURPOSE OF LIFE

When you know your destination, you know what to take along, what to leave and what is unnecessary. For example: If we are going to Shimla in December (winter), suppose we pack cotton clothing and go ,what will we be told ? It is ignorance and we are unintelligent to do something like this, people will ask us" Do you know where are you going and what are you carrying ?

Where is your Wisdom? And What will happen once you reach there? You anyway have to carry luggage, why not carry what is useful ? Carrying wrong luggage/weight is no point. What is destination of the soul ?

It will go through this lifetime in this costume. There will be a moment when the soul will leave this body and it takes a new costume. In that new costume what luggage carried from here will be useful for the soul ?

Sanskars, Nature, deeds, karmas so we know what will be useful for us in our future journey. So when we know what will be useful, we will need to take care.

At every point our vibrations creates the reality. Vibrations creates our reality is an equation which we need to remember.

We should not look at reality and create thoughts and words accordingly. What ever reality we want is what we should think and speak.

Once this equation gets fit within, we will create miracles so never curse a child. Blessings and curse both works. What is the reality you want for a child, Successful happy healthy ??

Start creating those vibrations for the child.

Blessings !! blessings !! blessings !!

Worry, anxiety, fear or insecurity about the child are opposite of Blessings.

"That I think so much. But do I think about what exactly I think ?

So

Purpose of life is....

a. *Living for thinking restlessly*
b. *Thinking for Living peacefully.*

Purpose of life is to live fully, totally- with total involvement.

Before you fall dead you should know every aspect of life.

CHAPTER TEN

Burning Desire Plus Detachment from Outcome

Everything is dual, everything is and isn't at the same time ,all truths are but half truths and every truth is half false, there are two sides to everything.

Ever lasting success is one out come after another while enjoying the journey. Joy of journey is to be present in the now that is how one achieves flow.

Reality is nothing but projection of our subconscious mind.To experience flow, you have to have burning desire and deattachment from outcome

What is better ?

Enjoying the journey or the outcome destination.?

What is flow ?

Flow is a state when challenge meets skills where the outcome and journey becomes one. Most information is stored in our subconscious mind. And reality is nothing but projection of our subconscious mind.

Discipline comes through self –control.

If you do not conquer self, you will be conquered by self.

You may see at one and same time both your best friend and your greatest enemy by stepping in front of a mirrior.

All negativity is caused by accumulation of psychological time and denial of the present.

Uneasiness ,anxiety ,tension, stress, worry-all forms of fear are caused by too much future and not enough presence.

Guilt, regret, resentment, grievances, sadness, bitterness and all forms of non forgiveness are caused by too much past and not enough presence.

“ one day I’ll make it “. Is your goal taking up so much of your attention that you reduce the present moment to a means to an end. Is it taking the joy out of your doing. Are you waiting to start living. If you deserve such a mind pattern, no matter what, you achieve or get, the present will never be good enough, the future will always seem better.A perfect reciepe for permanent dissatisfaction and non fulfillment, don’t you agree ?

That’s why one should go more deeply into NOW. That is the state where flow begins and miracle is created.

CHAPTER ELEVEN

WHO ARE WE ?

We are not aware of oushelves, we get this life as golden chance

How should we know, how great we are ?

That's why universe was made .Everything is splitted into two.Day and night, sad and happiness,hot and cold, left and right, life nad death.

Law of duality !!

We can not experience good till we experience bad.

So everything is important for existence.

Its upto us where we flow and we will have life experiences accordingly !!

सुना क्या

www.ingramcontent.com/pod-product-compliance
Ingram Content Group UK Ltd.
Pitfield, Milton Keynes, MK11 3LW, UK
UKHW060358300726
14090UKWH00001B/3

* 9 7 9 8 8 8 5 4 6 8 9 1 6 *